PIANO · VOCAL

ONLY HEAVEN

MUSIC OF RICKY IAN GORDON

ISBN 978-0-7935-8518-2

WILLIAMSON MUSIC®

A Division of The Rodgers & Hammerstein Organization:
A Concord Music Company

EXCLUSIVELY DISTRIBUTED BY

HAL•LEONARD®
7777 W. BLUEMOUND RD. P.O. BOX 13819 MILWAUKEE, WI 53213

For all works contained herein:
Unauthorized copying, arranging, adapting, recording or public performance is an infringement of copyright.
Infringers are liable under the law.

Williamson Music is a registered trademark used under license from Rodgers and Hammerstein.

MUSIC OF RICKY IAN GORDON

For
Jeffrey Michael Grossi
March 10, 1964 - August 1, 1996

ONLY HEAVEN

February 2, 1997
about the songs from *Only Heaven*

After I completed *Genius Child,* my cycle of ten songs using poems by Langston Hughes for high voice – commissioned by Harolyn Blackwell – I felt like I had only just begun my journey with Langston Hughes. These poems leap off the page at me with their economy of means, their internal rhythms, their ecstasies, and their depths. I had just finished doing a piece in Philadelphia, *States Of Independence,* for The American Music Theatre Festival with Writer/Director Tina Landau in the spring of 1993. It was a big exhausting piece which had to be written quickly (much of it in a hotel room, to be ready the next day) so when I returned home – it was these songs which pulled me back into writing. I practically wrote one a day for a while. I would get up and pick a poem according to how I was feeling and what was going on for me at the time. For example, after seeing a screening of Louis Malle's moody film *Le Feu Follet,* (The Fire Within) about the last days of a man tumbling toward suicide – wherein Malle uses Satie's Gymnopedies as the score, I wrote *Late Last Night.* I wrote*Stars* for my partner Jeffrey Grossi, who at that time had begun alternative physical, spiritual and mental treatments for dealing with his compromised immune system. He needed enormous strength and support and I suppose I wrote this song to give it to him. *Port Town,* I wrote while visiting my parents on their little ranch in Florida. The strange menagerie of animals, the balmy breezes and the swaying palm trees, all contribute to the playful yet slightly turgid atmosphere of the song. In the spring of 1995, I compiled these songs, along with some from *Genius Child,* into a theatre piece entitled *Only Heaven.* The title comes from the poem, *Luck,* – "to some people, love is given. To others, only heaven." Nancy Rhodes, Jack Gaughn, and their Encompass Music Theatre produced it (Nancy directed) with three wonderful singers, Sherry Boone, Michael Lofton and Theresa Hamm Smith. Mitchell Cirker conducted a little band from the piano, and USA Today said, *"The most distinctive music heard all season, it embraces Hughes' bumpy asymmetrical rhythms with a soaring mellifluousness, not bothering with catchy melodic hooks but going straight to the emotional center."*

This is a compilation of certain songs used in *Only Heaven,* certain others have previously been published in *Genius Child.* In some instances, where, in the show, they were duets or trios, I have restored them to their original status as solos.

On August 1, 1996 – last summer – Jeffrey Michael Grossi – I am sure – went straight into the light where Angels and Saints go. I dedicate this collection to him.

MUSIC OF RICKY IAN GORDON

HARLEM NIGHT SONG

Music by RICKY IAN GORDON
Text by LANGSTON HUGHES

Copyright © 1997 by Ricky Ian Gordon
Public Doves Music owner of publication and allied rights throughout the world (administered by Williamson Music)
International Copyright Secured   All Rights Reserved
Text by Langston Hughes
Copyright © 1994 by Alfred A. Knopf

8

DAYBREAK IN ALABAMA

Music by RICKY IAN GORDON
Text by LANGSTON HUGHES

Copyright © 1997 by Ricky Ian Gordon
Public Doves Music owner of publication and allied rights throughout the world (administered by Williamson Music)
International Copyright Secured   All Rights Reserved
Text by Langston Hughes
Copyright © 1994 by Alfred A. Knopf

dew.

I'm gon - na

poco piu lento

p

rit.

put some tall, tall trees in it,

Tempo

mf

And the scent of pine need - les, And the

smell of red clay af - ter rain, And

WHEN SUE WEARS RED

Music by RICKY IAN GORDON
Text by LANGSTON HUGHES

Copyright © 1997 by Ricky Ian Gordon
Public Doves Music owner of publication and allied rights throughout the world (administered by Williamson Music)
International Copyright Secured   All Rights Reserved
Text by Langston Hughes
Copyright © 1994 by Alfred A. Knopf

When Su - sa - na Jones _____ wears

LATE LAST NIGHT

Music by RICKY IAN GORDON
Text by LANGSTON HUGHES

Copyright © 1997 by Ricky Ian Gordon
Public Doves Music owner of publication and allied rights throughout the world (administered by Williamson Music)
International Copyright Secured   All Rights Reserved
Text by Langston Hughes
Copyright © 1994 by Alfred A. Knopf

I was cry - in' on ac -

count of you.

PORT TOWN

Music by RICKY IAN GORDON
Text by LANGSTON HUGHES

Copyright © 1997 by Ricky Ian Gordon
Public Doves Music owner of publication and allied rights throughout the world (administered by Williamson Music)
International Copyright Secured   All Rights Reserved
Text by Langston Hughes
Copyright © 1994 by Alfred A. Knopf

Hel - lo sail - or come___ with me.___

Come on, drink cog - nac, rath - er have wine.___

— Come here, I love you.___ Come and be

mine.

Come____ with me.____

DELINQUENT

Music by RICKY IAN GORDON
Text by LANGSTON HUGHES

Copyright © 1997 by Ricky Ian Gordon
Public Doves Music owner of publication and allied rights throughout the world (administered by Williamson Music)
International Copyright Secured   All Rights Reserved
Text by Langston Hughes
Copyright © 1994 by Alfred A. Knopf

Lyrics:

A ti - ger, a li - on, and all owl in her eyes.

Lit - tle Ju - lie___ says she don't care, What she means is:___

No - bo - dy cares an - y - where,___

ANGEL WINGS

Music by RICKY IAN GORDON
Text by LANGSTON HUGHES

Copyright © 1997 by Ricky Ian Gordon
Public Doves Music owner of publication and allied rights throughout the world (administered by Williamson Music)
International Copyright Secured   All Rights Reserved
Text by Langston Hughes
Copyright © 1994 by Alfred A. Knopf

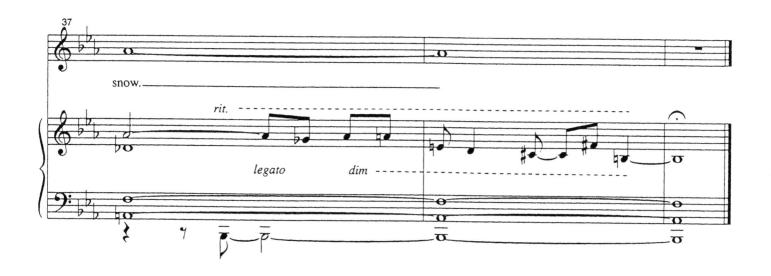

snow.

LUCK

Music by RICKY IAN GORDON
Text by LANGSTON HUGHES

Copyright © 1997 by Ricky Ian Gordon
Public Doves Music owner of publication and allied rights throughout the world (administered by Williamson Music)
International Copyright Secured   All Rights Reserved
Text by Langston Hughes
Copyright © 1994 by Alfred A. Knopf

some peo- ple.   Love   is   giv-en___

to   oth- ers___   On - ly   hea- ven.___

Dream Variations

Music by RICKY IAN GORDON
Text by LANGSTON HUGHES

Copyright © 1997 by Ricky Ian Gordon
Public Doves Music owner of publication and allied rights throughout the world (administered by Williamson Music)
International Copyright Secured   All Rights Reserved
Text by Langston Hughes
Copyright © 1994 by Alfred A. Knopf

STARS

Music by RICKY IAN GORDON
Text by LANGSTON HUGHES

Copyright © 1997 by Ricky Ian Gordon
Public Doves Music owner of publication and allied rights throughout the world (administered by Williamson Music)
International Copyright Secured   All Rights Reserved
Text by Langston Hughes
Copyright © 1994 by Alfred A. Knopf

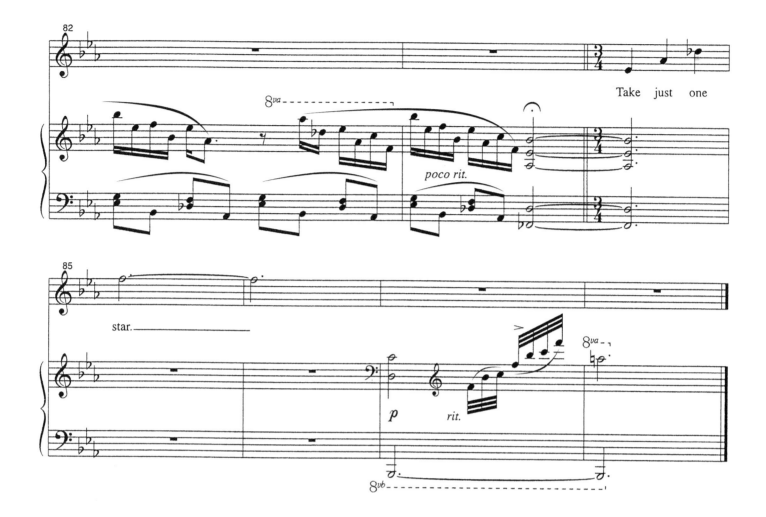

Take just one

star.

IN TIME OF SILVER RAIN

Music by RICKY IAN GORDON
Text by LANGSTON HUGHES

Copyright © 1997 by Ricky Ian Gordon
Public Doves Music owner of publication and allied rights throughout the world (administered by Williamson Music)
International Copyright Secured   All Rights Reserved
Text by Langston Hughes
Copyright © 1994 by Alfred A. Knopf

life.

slightly slower

rit.

DREAM

Music by RICKY IAN GORDON
Text by LANGSTON HUGHES

Copyright © 1997 by Ricky Ian Gordon
Public Doves Music owner of publication and allied rights throughout the world (administered by Williamson Music)
International Copyright Secured   All Rights Reserved
Text by Langston Hughes
Copyright © 1994 by Alfred A. Knopf

58

touched   you_____   a - sleep,_____

Face   to   the   wall,   I   said,

"How   dreams   can   lie,"_____   But   you_____   were   not

there   at   all._____

SONG FOR A DARK GIRL

Music by RICKY IAN GORDON
Text by LANGSTON HUGHES

Blues - desolate ♩. = 58

Way down south in Dixie,

Break the heart of me, *They hung my black young*

lover To a cross-roads tree.

Copyright © 1997 by Ricky Ian Gordon
Public Doves Music owner of publication and allied rights throughout the world (administered by Williamson Music)
International Copyright Secured   All Rights Reserved
Text by Langston Hughes
Copyright © 1994 by Alfred A. Knopf

Break the heart___ of me,___ Love___ is a

cresc.

ff

na - ked sha - dow___

mp

mf

rit.

poco piu lento

pp

on___ a gnar - led___ and___ na - ked___ tree.___

Tempo

rit.

DRUM

Music by RICKY IAN GORDON
Text by LANGSTON HUGHES

Copyright © 1997 by Ricky Ian Gordon
Public Doves Music owner of publication and allied rights throughout the world (administered by Williamson Music)
International Copyright Secured   All Rights Reserved
Text by Langston Hughes
Copyright © 1994 by Alfred A. Knopf

ev - er, Till the last worms_____ come to an - swer its__

- call,_____ Till the last stars_____ fall,_____ Un - til the

last a - tom is no a - tom at all,

decresc.

67

Un - til__ time is lost and there__ is no air, And space it - self is nothing no - where.__ Death__ is a drum, a sig - nal drum,__ call - ing

poco a poco cresc.

pp

sfz

now   to   come!   Come!   Come!_____

____ Death___ is   a   drum,   a   sig - nal

drum_____   call - ing   now   to

come!   Come!   Come!_____

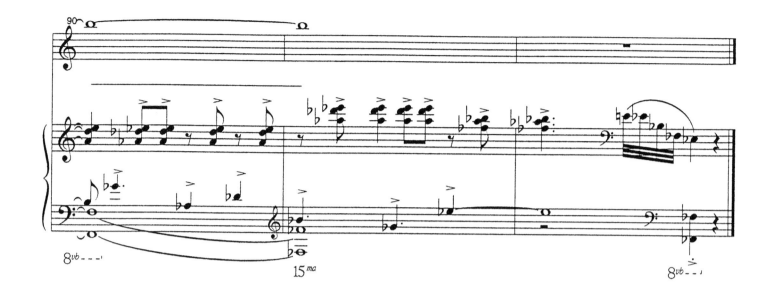

LITANY

Music by RICKY IAN GORDON
Text by LANGSTON HUGHES

Copyright © 1997 by Ricky Ian Gordon
Public Doves Music owner of publication and allied rights throughout the world (administered by Williamson Music)
International Copyright Secured   All Rights Reserved
Text by Langston Hughes
Copyright © 1994 by Alfred A. Knopf

Gath - er up in the arms of your pi - ty the sick, the de -

praved, the des - per - ate, the tired, all the scum of our

wea - ry ci - ty. Gath - er up in the arms of your pi - ty,

Gath - er up in the arms of your love those who ex -

pect   no   love_____   from   a -

(Roll chords when necessary)

bove._____

espressivo

mf   *dim.*   *p*

mf   *cresc.*

sub. pp   cresc.

wea - ry ci - ty. Gath - er up in the arms of your pi - ty,

Gath - er up in the arms of your love

those who ex - pect no love from a - bove.

NIGHT: FOUR SONGS

Music by RICKY IAN GORDON
Text by LANGSTON HUGHES

Copyright © 1997 by Ricky Ian Gordon
Public Doves Music owner of publication and allied rights throughout the world (administered by Williamson Music)
International Copyright Secured   All Rights Reserved
Text by Langston Hughes
Copyright © 1994 by Alfred A. Knopf

DEMAND

Music by RICKY IAN GORDON
Text by LANGSTON HUGHES

Copyright © 1997 by Ricky Ian Gordon
Public Doves Music owner of publication and allied rights throughout the world (administered by Williamson Music)
International Copyright Secured   All Rights Reserved
Text by Langston Hughes
Copyright © 1994 by Alfred A. Knopf

your bright breath.

Tell me dream

of ut - ter a - live - ness,

Know - ing so well the wind

RICKY IAN GORDON

BIOGRAPHY

Ricky Ian Gordon (b. 1956 in Oceanside, NY) studied piano, composition and acting, at Carnegie Mellon University. After moving to New York City, he quickly emerged as a leading writer of vocal music that spans art song, opera, and musical theater. Mr. Gordon's songs have been performed and or recorded by such internationally renowned singers as Renee Fleming, Dawn Upshaw, Nathan Gunn, Judy Collins, Nadine Sierra, Kelli O'Hara, Audra MacDonald, Kristin Chenoweth, Nicole Cabell, Frederica Von Stade, Andrea Marcovicci, Harolyn Blackwell, Betty Buckley, and the late Lorraine Hunt Lieberson, among many others.

Ricky Ian Gordon's most recent premieres include *The House Without A Christmas Tree* (2017, libretto by Royce Vavrek, commissioned and premiered by Houston Grand Opera) a holiday opera for young audiences that *The Wall Street Journal* describes as "a charming, family-friendly piece," and a reduction of *The Grapes of Wrath* (2017 two-act version commissioned and premiered by the Opera Theatre of St. Louis) which the Chicago Tribune calls "a great American opera."

A highly prolific composer, Ricky Ian Gordon's catalog also includes *Morning Star* (2015, libretto by William Hoffman, premiered by the Cincinnati Opera) about Jewish immigrants in New York's Lower East Side in the beginning of the 20th century; *27* (2014, libretto by Royce Vavrek, premiered at Opera Theatre of St. Louis) about Gertrude Stein's salons with Alice B. Toklas, at 27 rue de Fleurus; *A Coffin In Egypt* (2014, libretto by Leonard Foglia, premiered by the Houston Grand Opera, The Wallis Annenberg Center for the Performing Arts, and Opera Philadelphia) a haunting tale of memory and murder, racism and recrimination; *Rappahannock County* (2011, libretto by Mark Campbell, premiered at the Harrison Opera House) inspired by diaries, letters, and personal accounts from the Civil War in the 1860s; *Sycamore Trees* (2010, libretto by composer, premiered at The Signature Theatre) a musical about suburban secrets and family imbroglios; *The Grapes of Wrath* (2007 and 2010, libretto by Michael Korie, 2007 premiere by the Minnesota Opera, 2010 premiered by The American Symphony Orchestra); *Green Sneakers* (2008, libretto by the composer, premiered by the Miami String Quartet at Bravo! Vail Valley Music Festival) a theatrical song cycle for Baritone, String Quartet, and Empty Chair; *Orpheus and Euridice* (2005, libretto by composer, premiered by The Lincoln Center for the Performing Arts, Rose Theater); *My Life with Albertine* (2003, with Playwright Richard Nelson, premiered by Playwrights Horizons); *Night Flight To San Francisco* and *Antarctica* (2000) from Tony Kushner's *Angels In America*; *Dream True* (1999, with writer/director Tina Landau, premiered Vineyard Theater); *States Of Independence* (1992, with writer/director Tina Landau, premiered by The American Music Theater Festival); *The Tibetan Book of the Dead* (1996, libretto by Jean Claude van Itallie, premiered by Houston Grand Opera); *Only Heaven* (1995, libretto by Langston Hughes, premiered by Encompass Opera).

Upcoming projects include: the opera *Intimate Apparel* with playwright Lynn Nottage, commissioned by New York's Metropolitan Opera and Lincoln Center Theater; *Private Confessions* with playwright Richard Nelson, commissioned by The Goodman Theater in Chicago; *Ellen West* (libretto by Frank Bidart) commissioned by Beth Morrison Projects for a 2019 premiere; and, an opera based on Giorgio Bassani's novel *The Garden of the Finzi Continis* with librettist Michael Korie.

Mr. Gordon has been a visiting professor at colleges and universities throughout the country including Yale, NYU, Northwestern, Juilliard, Manhattan School of Music, Bennington, Vassar, Carnegie-Mellon, Elon, Michigan State, University of Michigan, Point Park (McGinnis Distinguished Lecturer), Texas Lutheran University, Eastman School of Music, Florida State University, Texas Christian University, and San Francisco Conservatory. He has been the featured Composer-in-Residence at Bravo! Vail Valley Music Festival, The Hawaii Performing Arts Festival, The Van Cliburn Foundation, Voices of Change, Santa Fe Song Festival, Songfest at Pepperdine University, Chautauqua, Aspen Music Festival, and Ravinia.

Among his honors are an OBIE Award, the 2003 Alumni Merit Award for exceptional achievement and leadership from Carnegie-Mellon University, A Shen Family Foundation Award, the Stephen Sondheim Award, The Gilman and Gonzalez-Falla Theater Foundation Award, The Constance Klinsky Award, The National Endowment of the Arts, The American Music Center, and many awards from ASCAP, of which he is a member.

Mr. Gordon's works are published by Williamson Music, Carl Fischer Music, and Theodore Presser Company and available everywhere.

His works are also widely recorded on various labels.